OAK BONES

POEMS BY
JIM GRONVOLD

OAK BONES

POEMS BY

JIM GRONVOLD

Oak Ink Press
2016

Copyright © 2015 Jim Gronvold
Revised edition 2016
All rights reserved

ISBN-10: 0692290222
ISBN-13: 978-0-692-29022-4

Book design: Wordsworth, San Geronimo, CA
Cover photo: Jim Gronvold

To order additional copies of *Oak Bones* or to contact the author, write:

>Oak Ink Press
>oakinkpress@icloud.com

To Ann
for her sweet support
and wise suggestions.

Contents

Dunlin Swarm	1
Stream	2
Shine	3
Simple	4
Old Big Sur	5
Dancers	6
Rain	7
Roadside	8
Grow	9
Shrine	10
Great Sky	11
Old Oak	12
Paradise	13
Music	14
Oak Bones	15
Warming	16
Coast Live Oak	17
Patchwork Sky	18
Humming Bird	19
Kestrel	20

House Sparrow	21
Thread	22
Cypress Bluff	23
River Drift	24
Description	25
True Nature	26
Alder Bark	27
Before	28
Great Mystery	29
Elements	30
Space	31
Patterns	32
Connection	33
Age Rings	34
Reactions	35
Egos	36
Corporate Gardens	37
More	38
Claims	39
Crust	40
Star Shells	41
Dune	42
Passing	43

Strangers	44
Now	45
Mirrors	46
All Names	47
Carved Angels	48
Dark Ages	49
Could	50
Divinity	51
Distraction	52
Reality	53
Spirit	54
Evolving	55
Share	56
Market Street	57
Trace	58
Bridge	59
Breath	60
We	61
Life	62
Garden	63
Waiting	64
America's Cup 2013	65
Pier 7	66

Larkspur Ferry	67
Norway	68
Buried Treasure	69
Morning Moon	70
Night Port	71
Marsh Ice	72
Ferns	73
Writing Poems	74
Dylan Thomas	75
Elder	76
Dear Departed	77
Everywhere	78
The Whole Shebang	79
Tea	80

Dunlin Swarm

Thousands of birds in a Dunlin cloud
rise from the muddy shallows

into slithering dragon silhouettes
that spin silver as they slide

over the winding shore
and shimmer into giant billows

turning inside out, rolling side to side
seeming to vanish before the sky

then suddenly flash a massive swirl
of twisting sunlit scales

that climb, dive and glide
back and forth beside the bay

until they fold a final curl
and furl like falling sails.

Stream

The stream we share
with all flowing things
strums the sky
and rattles the air

drums jungles
while deserts sigh

shakes forests
as lakes leap up
and deep oceans fly.

Tides turn and terns reel
seasons roll round our wheel.

Leaves green down
to gold and brown
in silent currents
that crash and sing
the elements of everywhere
and every rippling thing.

Shine

Oceans rush through our veins
lightning drives our dreams

everything evaporating
shares our family tree.

Leaves stir into soil
breath swirls into wind

blood drifts into cloud
and returns to Earth in rain

splashing on rolling seas,
hillsides and dusty planes

wetting the shiny skin
of this tiny spinning grain

that sparkles in a mist
of billions of scattered stars.

Simple

Reverence for Nature
is a simple thing

it's touching a breeze
that feels like Spring

or listening to
a sparrow or starling.

It's stopping to watch
ripples of sunrise

or standing in awe
of deep night skies

it's our interest in
all natural things

with or without words
to give our wonder wings.

Old Big Sur

Swift shallow water
tumbling over stones
turns spinning bubbles
into sweet sound

on a river as clear
as rippling crystal
flowing through itself—
ocean bound.

And web-rooted
redwoods tower
over quiet trails
and wildflower

while breaking waves
dash sculpted shores
explored by otters
and soaring condors.

Grand and intimate
wonders stir
wherever you look
at the wild edges
of roaring old Big Sur.

Dancers

Two thin-skinned beauties
of the western hills

the smooth-veiled
Manzanita
and the cinnamon-scaled
Madrone

calmly swing their
twisting shadows
to the slow beat of the Sun

and barely turning
are fairly spun
by rhythms
that seasons compose.

Rain

The seething pulse
of dirt and sky

wears many skins
that seed the wind

and feed the soil
that daylight spins.

The beating ocean
forges cloud

turning its blood
into rivers

that churn into
fertile mud

opening leaf
and willow bud.

Roadside

Roadside flowers
blue and gold
hold my bending attention

and draw me into
their green fold
with tiny shapes
of simple perfection

that dance at the edge
of asphalt
crawling in every direction.

Grow

Acorns fall
before they climb
back into tall trees.

Waters rise into cloud
until they spill
and fill a breeze.

Life awakens anywhere
conditions may allow

grow, decay, fall or fly
it all continues
somewhere, somehow.

Shrine

Kneeling to tie a shoe
at the crumbling shrine
of a fallen tree
on an altar of quiet hill

I lace my feet to the path
of the sacred oak and pine.
To the hawk, the dove and deer
that grace the green divine.

Great Sky

The Great Sky
whose breath is the wind
whose blood is the rain

beats the drum in my chest
and lifts my wings again.

The Great River
whose ghost is cloud
whose tribe is the sea

carries the Sun on ripple stars
that float along with me.

The Great Mountain
with feet on plains
and drifting fingers of sand

holds me by my roots
and sows me over fertile land.

Old Oak

The calm presence
of an ancient oak
on a stark
and windy hill

standing through
every weather

reminds me
to just stand still
and simply be
the space I fill.

Paradise

Under an oak
of great height

I squint at the Sun
stepping down leaves

as paradise falls
through their shade

in a slow cascade
of sparkling light,

glimmering halos
and sliding prisms

descending rungs
of leafy branches

into the shadows
of rising night.

Jim Gronvold

Music

There is sacred music
in the wings of trees

and we are some
of the chattering leaves

that sing the breeze
that rubs us together—

whispers in
the forest of stars.

Oak Bones

Forested centuries
of giant trees
brought to their knees
by ax and saw
for sailing ships
and factories—
buildings,
barrels and tables.

For oak bone
railroad ties
that connected
cities by steel
but tore apart
ancient forests
with wounds
that may never heal.

Jim Gronvold

Warming

In a straw gold clearing
bound by shade

and speckled borders
spotted with deer

soft morning colors
begin to fade

in a warming day
of another dry year

in another ever
drier decade

under our burning
atmosphere.

Coast Live Oak

Oak limbs lean against a slope
where wandering cattle stray
among the sprawling Buckeye
and the California Bay
which spreads the Live Oak virus
of sudden death and slow decay.

Trees that fed ancestral tribes
with acorn meal ground on stone
still nourish quail and deer
until they fall, turn pale as bone
and slowly disappear.

Patchwork Sky

Starlings sweep a patchwork sky
stitched by sparrow and crow.

Red-tailed hawks spin their spools
and fade into the denim blue.

Hummingbirds sew bright buttons
on woven tangles of rising vines

until wild geese press formal lines
and crease the wide unwinding.

Humming Bird

With a flash of brilliance
and a quick tongue

this cloud-winged hummer
and preacher of the Sun

skims the simmering
brush of summer

bearing his shimmering
scroll of light

on a spark burst
sliding out of sight.

Kestrel

A kestrel curls the shore in his wings
and stays afloat above a hill
by stuffing air in his pockets
and almost standing still.

Anchored to a shadow
in the mouse-grass
under his steady gaze
he flutters in place
for a long while
treading the air in silence

then, with great patience and skill
he freezes on a moment
and dives to the kill.

House Sparrow

Just a sparrow face in the crowd
another beak at the feeder.

A chip off the old flock
thinking out loud
chirping away
in the din of chatter.

At night in the park
in the quiet dark
when he's fluffed
his feathers
and tucked his wings

does he close his eyes
and chirp in his sleep
or sing in mumbling clatter?

Thread

A silk strand across blue sky—
the vapor trail of a small spider
floating a hundred feet high.

Tethered to a towering tree
she threw herself onto the wind
to find a better place for prey
but at the end of her nimble thread
might drift too far and land in the bay.

Cypress Bluff

From the shade
of a cypress window

on armchair roots
at the frayed edge
of a steep and rocky grade

we watch otters
on the surf below
roll off their backs
shadow through waves
and slip to the surface
between the rows

as we sip tea under the boughs
in whispers of ocean echo.

Jim Gronvold

River Drift

For all of its brilliant beauty
this golden blue hilltop view
of light-fall on water

might only be a footprint
of drifting time passing through
on its way to nowhere but here.

Description

By noon the trees
pulled their shadows in.

Or did the Sun
crawl into their shade?

Were those dark patches
only shrinking

or did Night and Day
work out a trade?

How soon the
painting mind will find

words that could
drive it colorblind

from all the
effort of thinking.

Jim Gronvold

True Nature

In blue contemplation
of ocean and sky

the true nature
of sunlight will shine

but the need for words
may not be clear

when cloud and wave define
the wild nature of our sphere.

Alder Bark

Those pinch-faced scars on alder bark
the heavy eyelids and puckered lips

are portrait parts out-of-place
on unintentional totem poles

that might have sparked folk tales
of talking trees and captive souls

for those who saw their own face
in nature's many veils.

Before

Before the arts of calculation
infinity equaled zero

wolves howled at the moon
and sagas grew in its glow.

Before science fiction
became what we know

myth led our scattered tribes
as far as faith could go

before we caught our breath
and let the rivers flow.

Great Mystery

What set the spark
that split the night
at the point of
deepest mystery?

What sort of storm
spun billions of suns
out of gas and dust
into radiant light?

And what chain reaction
of fortune or favor
created creatures
who would even ask?

Elements

Elements connected
by chance
and collected
by repeated circumstance

arrange their own reality
with unintentional elegance

revealing the true complexity
of natural consequence.

Space

From the subatomic
to the far unseen

movement is born
in the space between

specks and stars
with room to fly

that may collide
in the womb of space

divide and bloom
or crash and die

or simply vanish
without a trace.

Patterns

In the complex dance
of cause and effect

patterns formed
by trial or chance

tune intuition
and common sense

in moments of recognition
that inspire songs of science.

Connection

The weaver of weather
and every culture

the link between
past and future.

As a basic
condition of Nature

Cause and Effect
may be the dynamic

by which all things
could connect—

the spirit of
interaction

that deserves
our deepest respect.

Jim Gronvold

Age Rings

Age rings in trees
and wrinkles on shells

reflect echoes
of breaking swells

that wash the shores
that we all share

the way the ripples
we make when we speak

might not shake the air
like great brass bells

but could ring true,
if not unique.

Reactions

A silent cloud
a waterfall

a broken window
an open door

cause and effect
connect them all

from the push and pull of love
to the push and shove of war.

Passions ignite reactions
in ways we might not expect

as consequences we cause
continue to lead to more.

Egos

Spark flecks
of electric perception
struck by elegant accident

make new connections
repeat, combine

drift apart and realign
in patterns of
complex recognition

and see themselves
as the grand design
of all the scattered
suns that shine.

Corporate Gardens

Clock faces open
in plate-glass gardens

where digital numbers
fall like rain

and deadlines force
early bloomers

who blush and fade
under the strain

of grinding wheels
unwinding a spring

of roulette deals
ticking down

the numbered days
of their reign.

Jim Gronvold

More

Why do we think we need more
and trade our lives for the price

or need to dream of heaven
when we live on paradise?

Why can't the countdown of seasons
be reason enough to survive

or the pulse of any moment
be enough to feel alive?

Claims

We belong to the Earth
but buy and sell its land.

We belong to the sea
but stain its diamond sand.

We belong to the stars
but steal their light for dreams

that claim divine insight
but spark our dark extremes.

Crust

Everything crumbling
returns to compost

in recycle bins,
smoldering landfills

and mountains that crest
on the rolling crust

of this lava-filled pie
in the unfolding sky.

Star Shells

As only the shells of soul are seen
on sidewalks or sitting in cars,
on the clearest night we will only see
the shed skins of stars.

Those flickering phantom suns
threw off their light so long ago
that they are just the afterglow
of stars that may no longer burn
but still ignite our wonder.

If we shine on after we're gone
it may be as fading glimmers
in the memories of those
who have not let us go
but like the stars themselves
how would we ever know?

Dune

Climbing over
grass-feathered sand
to ocean as far
as I can see

I stretch my arms
to catch the air
from an edge of
the wide horizon

as the surf sighs
and skies expand
through my fingers
to everywhere.

Passing

Passing through
everything passing
on the way to
who-knows-where

I become aware
that change alone
is the one thing
that all things share.

And while our chances
rise or fall
we can savor
each breath of air

or allow the
impermanence
of it all
to open a door
that leads to despair.

Strangers

The lost poems of strangers
and the uncelebrated dead

shared feelings we might have known
in ways we may not have read.

Their thoughts haunt human memory
like shadows of unsown seed

with unheard words that whisper
between the lines we read.

Now

All that we do
we're doing right now

learning to walk
forgetting our names

testing what
limits allow

building, repairing
selling or stealing

harming or healing
breathing our last

being blessed
being cursed
taking a fall.

At our best
we stand
in awe of it all.

Mirrors

Facing our own mortality
as precious moments pass

we mirror-shards of reality
reflect on the nature of glass

constructing elaborate frames
for things we might have seen

inventing convincing names
for what we think they mean.

All Names

All names for the sacred
share the same sky
but tell separate stories.

All claims on heaven
split paradise
into rival territories.

And whatever we call
the mystery behind
all that we see and feel

the beauties of reality
are as sacred as they are real.

Jim Gronvold

Carved Angels

We searched the sky
for solid ground

worshiped words
we thought profound

and carved angels
out of stone

or gave the stars
flesh and bone

rather than face
the great unknown

and embrace
the only time we own.

Dark Ages

When dogmas
were quilled
by sword point
people retreated
to gilded clouds

or hid behind walls
of creed and crown
hoping that mercy
would one day rain down.

But those who
questioned authority
and would not be
coerced or bought
with promises of eternity

could die in dungeons
or burn at the stake
for the sake of free
expression and thought.

Jim Gronvold

Could

I could pray
for answers to fall

from a higher heaven
than a fine day—

or align myself
with the flowing way

of the changing
shape of it all.

Divinity

Peering into endless space
from a dot in infinity

or watching sunlight turn to green
and wither in my hand

is the simple kind of divinity
that I can understand.

Distraction

What better distraction than reality
to hold the future at bay

or tame the dreams that came true
but burn in the light of day?

What better escape than the present
from worries of tomorrow's pain

that paint their darkest past
and drown us in their stain?

Reality

Reality would be a religion
if it needed faith to be seen.

If it tried to enshrine
a mystical vision
with ritual ceremony

and defined the divine
in commanding terms
within a compelling story.

But reality seems to shine
in the light of observation

and shimmers in the shadow
of credible calculation.

Spirit

Spirit may be the energy
connecting body and mind

or the pulse of all activity
that we have yet to find.

Not for me the mythology
of riddles that will not unwind

nor sweet dreams of eternity
that mesmerize humankind

with shadows of the sorcery
that we have yet to leave behind.

Evolving

In the spirit
of deep connection
to everything
near and far

from the lives we brush
and places we know
to the hush
of a distant star

our curious minds
might outgrow
the dreams that
we think we are.

Jim Gronvold

Share

Whether spirit
scatters like smoke
or turns into ghosts
or ceases to be.

Whether we dissolve
into thin air
or suddenly stop
or are set free.

Whether or not
we go anywhere
right now we breathe
the heaven we share
for moments as rich
as they are rare.

Market Street

Walking up Market
on a day all my own

I was caught off guard
by the broken tone
of a brittle voice
that I might have known

holding a crumpled cup
to catch a little change.

I didn't know his name
or recognize his face
but I could smell
the bitter shame
of rotten luck and booze

that another time or place
might put me in his shoes.

Trace

Sometimes an edge
of mirror may show
on the face
of a total stranger

or you'll hear a trace
of your own echo—
in a voice that you
would never know—
express a feeling
that you have known
and always thought
was yours alone.

Bridge

Driving under towering arches
in late evening on the Golden Gate

with wind rushing through my windows
I steal a glance at the night-bright Bay

sparkling as it inhales the ocean
the way that stars take your breath away

and I feel caught in the swift current
of a narrow span of highway

but catch a breath of open sea
and float the sky that flows through me

between the rolling headlands
and the rising lights of the city.

Breath

Feelings only scratch
the skin of reality.

Instincts tend to simplify
life's complexity.

Thoughts try to understand.
Emotions seek intensity

and fantasy may design
dreams of eternity

but breath is the sweetest verse
a seeking mind may find.

We

We water, soil and sky
spun and spinning
ripple to ripple
falling as we fly.

We sons and daughters
leaves and bark
sand and spark
silence and cry.

We crumbs and crust
iron and rust
reason from chaos
and dreams out of dust.

We creatures who learned
to walk upright
and light fires
against the night

now launch ourselves
into flight
and read the history
of starlight.

Life

I'm as immortal
as memories of me

or a few dubious rumors
and ripples in a family tree

so myths of immortality
are hard for me to swallow

but Life itself is a story
that I am able to follow.

Garden

Not everyone
will ponder

how shadows fade
under passing Sun

or look beyond
beliefs undone

by the light
of observation

Waiting

Waiting for life to begin
is like betting your breath
on a prize after death
as if there were any to win.

Better to walk on solid ground
or sail a rolling sea
than to drift around spellbound
by a dream of bliss to be.

America's Cup 2013

Tall wing sails
beat the wind
right out of the gate

hulls leap out of
flying waters
on knife fin rudders
and daggerfoils
skating the chop
kicking up spray

they tack and attack
lift and dive
grinding across
the open Bay

round their marks
and wind it back
stitching up wind
between Alcatraz
and the rising cheers
of chattering crowds
on San Francisco piers.

Pier 7

A bridge connects place to place
but a pier connects to liquid space.

Fishermen shadows at the rail
haloed by sunrise waters
are deaf to the rush hour echo
of cars on the Embarcadero.

Baited hooks sink into the dark
to lure the shiny souls
that haunt the edge of currents
where deep water ships embark

while daydreaming fishermen
anchored to benches
drift on a harbor breeze
past ferryboats and freighters
to white-sand fantasies.

Larkspur Ferry

Late afternoon
all sparkles and bridges

commuters and sports fans
cling to the deck.

Whitecaps clap a steel hull
while jackets flap off shirts and skirts.

I'm at the rail like a car-window dog
hair flying out of my skull

when I'm splashed in the face
by a thin spray of gin
off a pin-stripe spilling his drink upwind

and that old taste almost triggers a thirst
but I just grin back into the wind.

Norway

Forever foreign
to these ancient shores,
to the old family's
sons and daughters

to the ancestors
who plowed these hills
and harvested these waters

I return a wandering weed
to the roots of my scattered seed

and feel my spirit restored
on the stone ruins
above the fjord.

Buried Treasure

The buried treasure
that I once found
was a sharpened stone
I pulled from the ground

a shard of flint
chipped to a shape
that someone used
to cut and scrape
meat from hide
for food and fur.

Its value now
is its connection
to forgotten faces
of a lost world
at the far root
of my own reflection

where it might have been
a common tool
to the last person who held it
but in my hand
it was a jewel
of solid human spirit.

Jim Gronvold

Morning Moon

Moon on a tightrope
between high-wire towers

dances on the edge
of Summer and Fall

then slips to the net
of shadow-hours

that in our turn
will catch us all.

Night Port

Aircraft circle the dance floor
asking for permission to land.

Boston's evening dress shimmers
and twinkling beacons wink.

Landing-light halos peek through cloud
and peer down a necklace skyline

as all the runway stars align
and spinning heals squeak on tarmac

then taxi to an airline hub
to the sound of high-pitch turbine.

Marsh Ice

Frozen scales of high water
drape the banks in sheets of ice—

shed skins of a snaking river
left behind by a shrinking tide

until the wandering ocean returns
and lifts the snow-lace veil from its bride.

Ferns

Ferns die back under killer frost
but survive in the heart of their roots.

The forest gardens we seem to have lost
will rise again when green shoots
uncurl and stretch their wide fronds
in the dappled shade of warmer sun

when ice has left the beaver ponds
and the fierce work of winter is done.

Jim Gronvold

Writing Poems

Quiet watching
written in whispers

searching out sounds
that might apply—

tapping the air
to tip the scales

in favor of
a truer line—

weighing the sky
against small words

for feelings as fine
as hummingbirds.

Dylan Thomas

Catching the drift
of fading light
a voice spun out
of the Welsh hills
rolled down stream
and slipped out of sight
to soar the heavens
of nevermore
forever on the tail
of a boy's frail kite
sailing the wide
other side of singing
with the echoes of birds
fallen into flight
among rising, falling,
upsetting suns
that wash the star-sanded
sea into night.

Elder

Child of it all
reptilian angel
wandering where you lie

your blood is the
dreaming dust of stars
your face a pool
of changing sky

your smile as soft
as memories
that return for a moment
to say goodbye.

Dear Departed

You're in the way I look at things
when I remember you

in leaf-shadow twilight
or cloud-reflecting dew.

You're in the passing wonder
of beating wings in flight

and part of all the sparkling suns
I ponder in the night.

Jim Gronvold

Everywhere

Could everywhere
be where we are
when we aren't
anywhere?

When we stop
fighting the current
or can't come up for air

do all our possibilities
end right then and there

or could we scatter on the sea
and sparkle in the glare?

The Whole Shebang

The universe is expanding
beyond my comprehension.

Will the vast burst of galaxies
fall like firework rain

or crash back through itself
on a starry tide down a cosmic drain

to a caldron of pure energy
and then blow itself up again?

The whole shebang
may be coming undone
but before the stars unscrew

I'll lean back as long as I can
and enjoy the unwinding view.

Tea

The simple wonder
of a green hill
changing shades
under turning sky.

The easy pace
of a cup of tea
in a quiet place
where time slips by

where clouds chase
the dust away
and a soaring
hawk may cry.

www.ingramcontent.com/pod-product-compliance
Lightning Source LLC
Chambersburg PA
CBHW072102290426

44110CB00014B/1796